Special Symbols:

This book is organized to guide the individual through the train...g. ... .
Notes section there are a number of symbols used to help the participant throughout the presentation and workshop. For your convenience these symbols are repeated at the introduction of each section of this workbook.

Suggestion:

This symbol represents a suggestion or is a general statement relating to facilitation of the training.

Tip:

This symbol represents a tip to the Facilitator and is specific to the concept that the Facilitator is presenting.

Question:

This symbol represents a question that may be asked to the Facilitator or to the participants in the workshop. It is intended to foster interaction during the training.

Table of Contents

Section 1

Section 2

Section 3

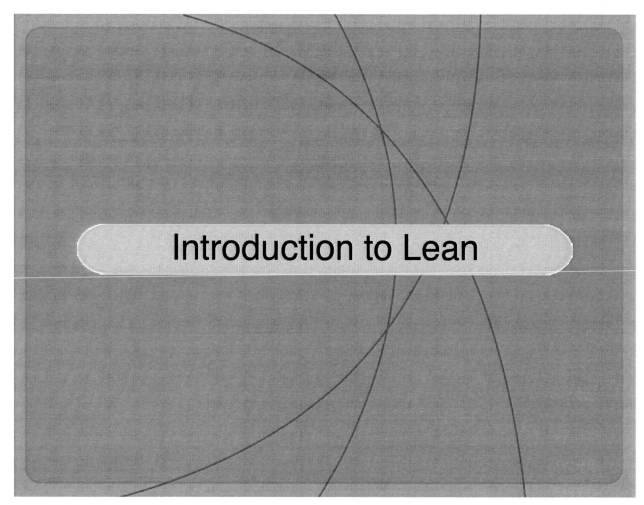

Introduction to Lean

Participant Workbook

In this Section

- Review the history of Lean & Learn Lean Methodology
- Study the components of Lean
- Understand the Workshop Content

Participant Workbook Provided To:

_____

 Suggestion   **Tip**   **Question**

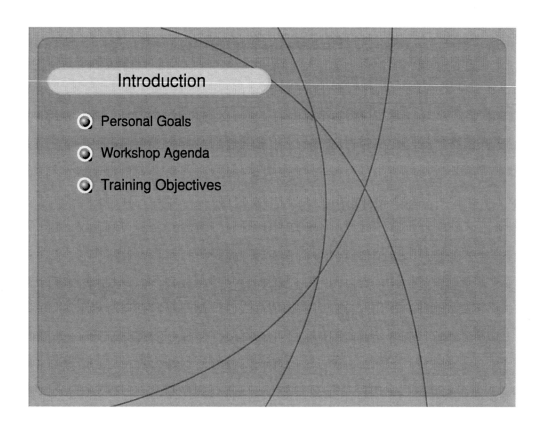

Introduction

- Personal Goals
- Workshop Agenda
- Training Objectives

Notes, Slide 2:

_____

_____

_____

_____

_____

_____

Tip:
As you go through this presentation, remember to stay focused on the general concepts and look for what is common to your experience, not what is different.

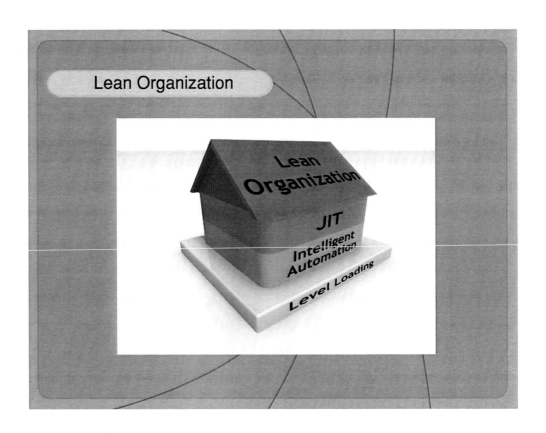

Notes, Slide 3:

_____

_____

_____

_____

_____

_____

Tip:
To understand how lean fits in your organization, ask the facilitator specific questions regarding the history of Lean.

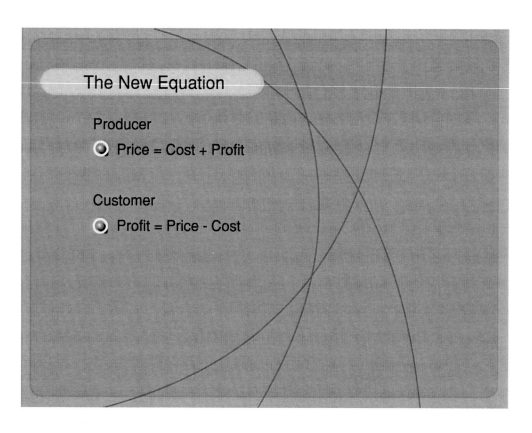

Notes, Slide 4:

_____

_____

_____

_____

_____

_____

What is Lean

A methodology that focuses on eliminating the 7 Wastes

Notes, Slide 5:

_____

_____

_____

_____

_____

_____

_____

Suggestion:
Be organized and prepared. Arrive early and be willing to engage the concepts.

Production Cycle Reduction

"One of the most noteworthy accomplishments in keeping the price of _____ products low is the gradual shortening of the production cycle. The longer an article is in the process of manufacture and the more it is moved about, the greater is its ultimate cost."

Who is being quoted here?
When was this said?

Notes, Slide 6:

_____

_____

_____

_____

_____

_____

Question:

Who is being quoted here? When was this said?

_____

_____

_____

History of Lean

- Lean's Birthplace: USA
  - 1900 est. Time & Motion Studied
  - 1913 Ford Production System established
- Lean first practiced in Japan
  - 1950's Dr. Demings Management System is studied
  - 1973 Toyota Production System
- Lean now world-wide
  - 1990's Starting in the USA
  - 2000+ Lean integrating into Corporate Strategies

Notes, Slide 7:

Tip:

Lean Manufacturing is a term credited to a gentleman named James P. Womack. He studied the Toyota Production System and co-authored a book entitled, "The Machine that Changed the World".

Lead-Time Reduction

- Quality & Time
  - Cost & Time
    - Deliver & Time
      - Safety & Time
        - Morale & Time

- QCDSM

Notes, Slide 8:

_____

_____

_____

_____

_____

Tip:

For an operation to be successful, we need to focus on the use of time in all respects. It is the only resource that we cannot get more of, and for this reason focusing on time will provide the best motivation for all other factors that are important to a business.

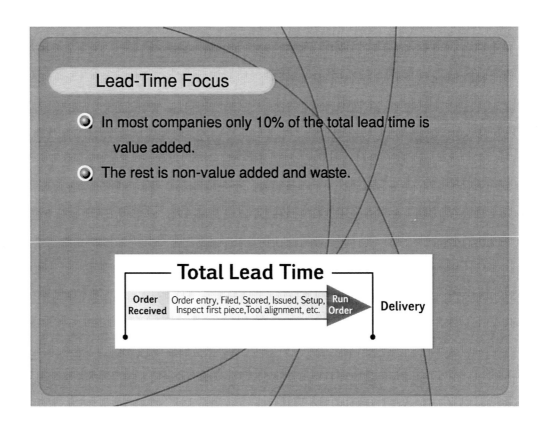

Notes, Slide 9:

Suggestion:
Ask questions when you feel clarification is needed.

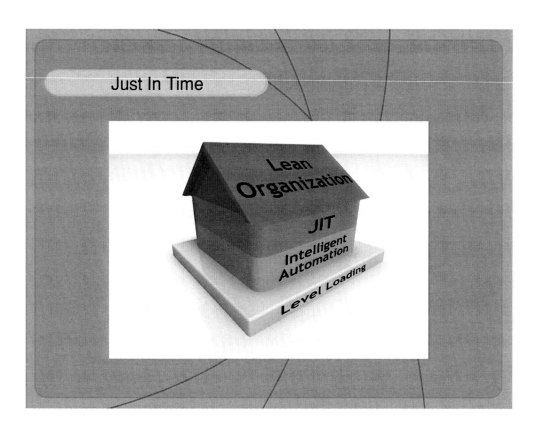

Notes, Slide 10:

_____

_____

_____

_____

_____

_____

Just In Time

- Making what the customer needs, when they need it, in the quantity needed

- Uses the least amount of effort, materials, equipment, machinery, and space to get the job done

- Exposes hidden problems and the 8 Wastes

- Just In Time is three principles:
    - Takt Time
    - Flow Production
    - Pull System

Notes, Slide 11:

_____

_____

_____

_____

_____

_____

Tip:

JIT Focuses on what the next customer needs in the process of manufacturing or processing information. If you are staisfying your next customer in your company then you are doing the right thing.

Question:

Just In Time is the result of what three factors?

_____

_____

_____

Takt Time

- The word "Takt" is German for the baton that an orchestra conductor uses to regulate the timing of a musical piece.

- In business, Takt Time is the "Beat Time" for operations set by the customer. It is the rate at which the customer buys products.

- Takt Time cannot be measured. Takt Time is only calculated.

Notes, Slide 12:

_____

_____

_____

_____

_____

Question:

What does Takt Time in operations stand for?

_____

_____

_____

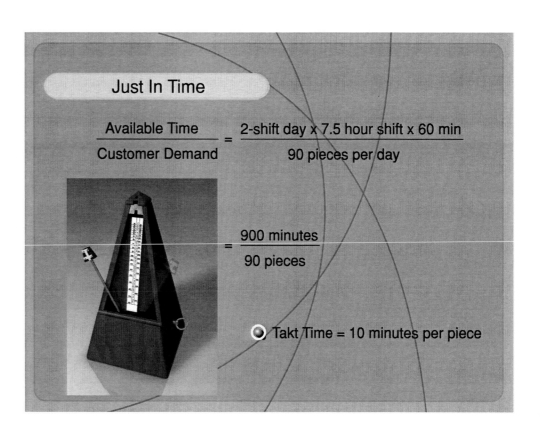

Just In Time

$$\frac{\text{Available Time}}{\text{Customer Demand}} = \frac{\text{2-shift day x 7.5 hour shift x 60 min}}{\text{90 pieces per day}}$$

$$= \frac{\text{900 minutes}}{\text{90 pieces}}$$

Takt Time = 10 minutes per piece

Notes, Slide 13:

_____

_____

_____

_____

_____

_____

_____

Tip:

One key concept in Lean or JIT is the end result of the equation of Takt Time. It is minutes per piece, not pieces per minute. This is the fundamental difference to calculating operations.

Balance based on Takt Time

- Takt Time only changes if customer demand or available time changes

- Balance all cycle times to Takt Time

Before Lean

Cycle Time (y-axis: 0, 2, 4, 6, 8, 10, 12)

Process Step: Form, Drill, Weld, Anodize, Assemble

After Lean

Cycle Time (y-axis: 0, 2, 4, 6, 8, 10, 12)

Process Step: Form & Drill, Drill, Drill, Weld & Anodize, Anodize & Assemble

Notes, Slide 14:

_____

_____

_____

_____

_____

_____

Question:

What are some of the benefits for balancing to Takt Time?

_____

_____

_____

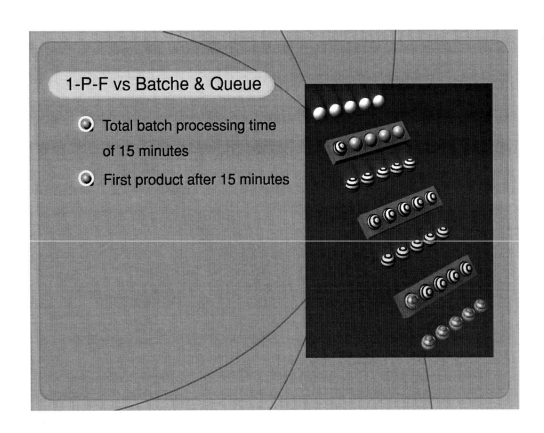

Notes, Slide 15:

Suggestion:
Ask the Facilitator to explain this concept as it is key to understanding the impact of batch production on the cost of operations.

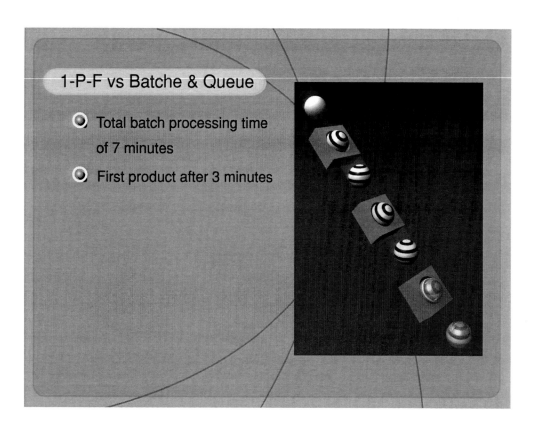

1-P-F vs Batche & Queue

- Total batch processing time of 7 minutes
- First product after 3 minutes

Notes, Slide 16:

Tip:
Notice that the change in these processes are the amount of inventory in process, the size of the staging areas, and the transportation between each stage. By going to a Lean operation, you can minimize those kinds of costs.

1-P-F Defined

- Moving product from one process to the next without waiting
  - Quality: Bad parts immediately apparent
  - Cost: Less Work-In-Process and space
  - Delivery: Shortest lead time
  - Safety: Less motion
  - Morale: Problems revealed sooner

Notes, Slide 17:

_____

_____

_____

_____

_____

_____

Question:

What are other benefits of One-Piece-Flow?

_____

_____

_____

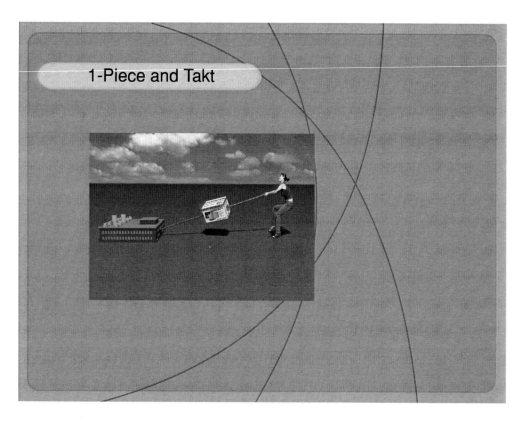

1-Piece and Takt

Notes, Slide 18:

_____

_____

_____

_____

_____

_____

Question:

What are the two kinds of customers for a company?

_____

_____

_____

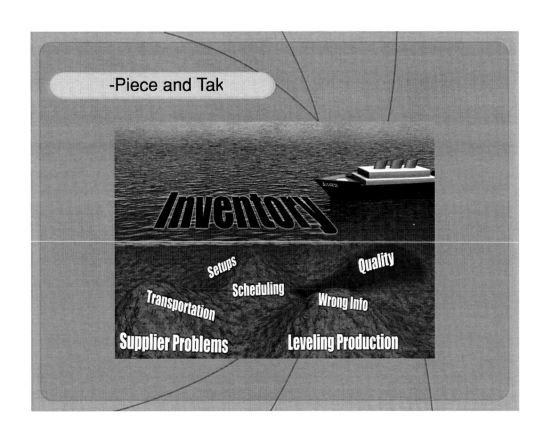

Notes, Slide 19:

Suggestion:

Engage the trainer on concepts that seem to be counter intuitive.

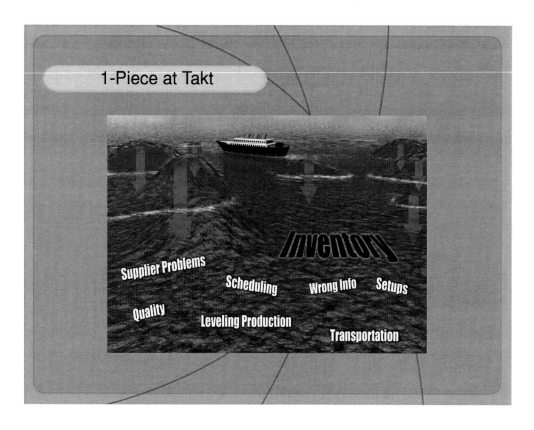

1-Piece at Takt

Notes, Slide 20:

_____

_____

_____

_____

_____

Question:

What rock in your department should be looked at first?

_____

_____

_____

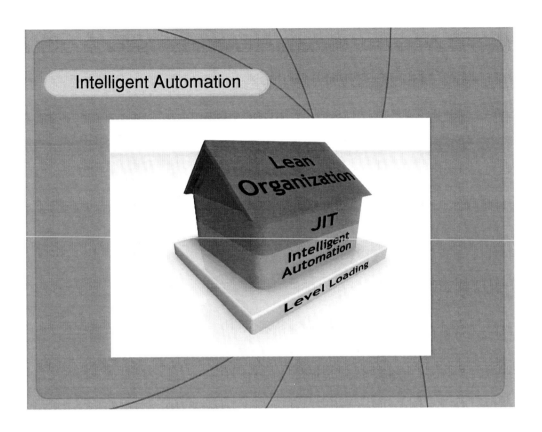

Notes, Slide 21:

_____

_____

_____

_____

_____

_____

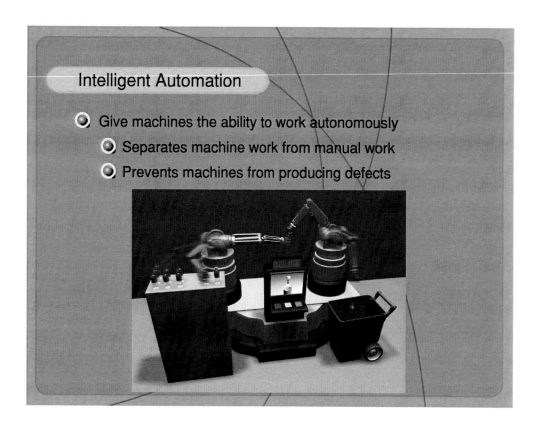

Intelligent Automation

- Give machines the ability to work autonomously
  - Separates machine work from manual work
  - Prevents machines from producing defects

Notes, Slide 22:

Tip:
Automating something does not mean that it is autonomous. For example, a car has automation components, but it is not autonomous to you needing to drive the vehicle.

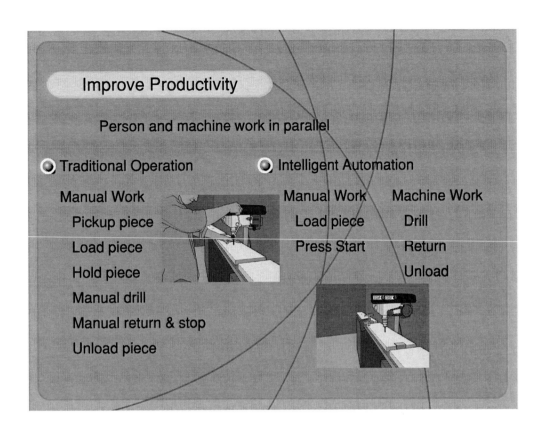

Improve Productivity

Person and machine work in parallel

◉ Traditional Operation   ◉ Intelligent Automation

Manual Work   Manual Work   Machine Work

  Pickup piece   Load piece   Drill

  Load piece   Press Start   Return

  Hold piece   Unload

  Manual drill

  Manual return & stop

  Unload piece

Notes, Slide 23:

Tip:

Think of intelligent automation as making many small steps towards the machine performing some taks without supervision. Maybe the first step is unloading a part.

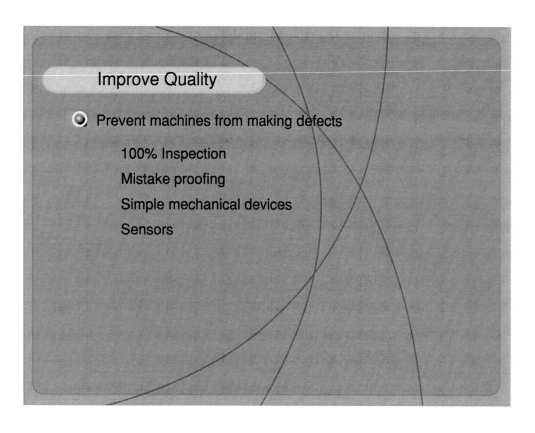

Notes, Slide 24:

_____

_____

_____

_____

_____

_____

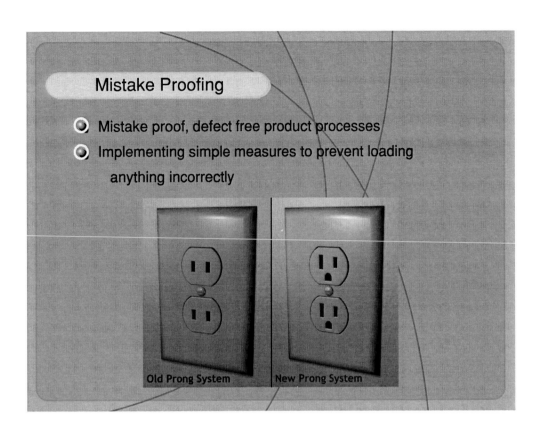

Mistake Proofing

- Mistake proof, defect free product processes
- Implementing simple measures to prevent loading anything incorrectly

Old Prong System   New Prong System

Notes, Slide 25:

Tip:
Think of a way to stop a machine or person from having the option of making a defect. This is the ultimate goal of mistake proofing.

Defect Prevention

- The goal is to mistake proof and prevent defects rather than shutting down a process after a defect is detected

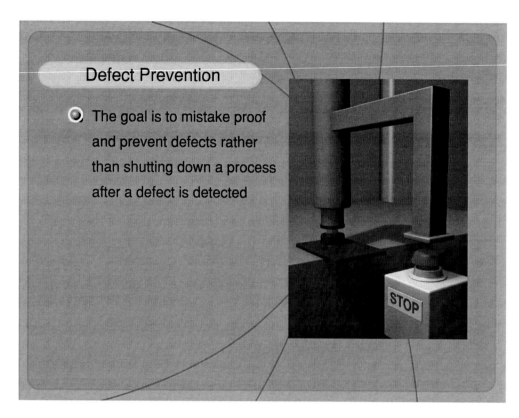

Tip:
As this illustration shows, there may be an easy way to prevent a defect from occurring.

Notes, Slide 26:

_____

_____

_____

_____

_____

_____

Question:
Is there an example of this in your area?

_____

_____

_____

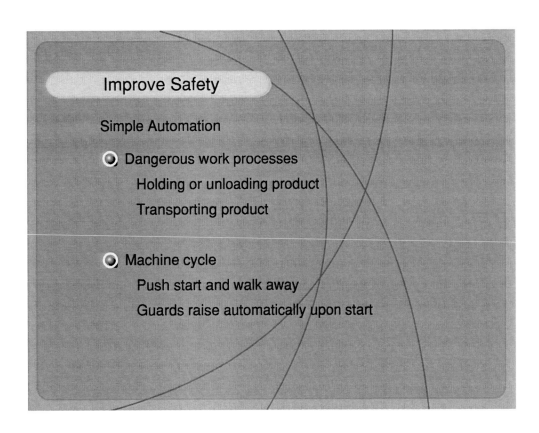

Notes, Slide 27:

_____

_____

_____

_____

_____

_____

Suggestion:

Think of ways to improve safety without having to spend too much money. This will allow the process of improving, in itself, flexible to change.

Level Loading

○ Balance production mix and volume to avoid excess inventory, uneven work pace, and capacity requirements

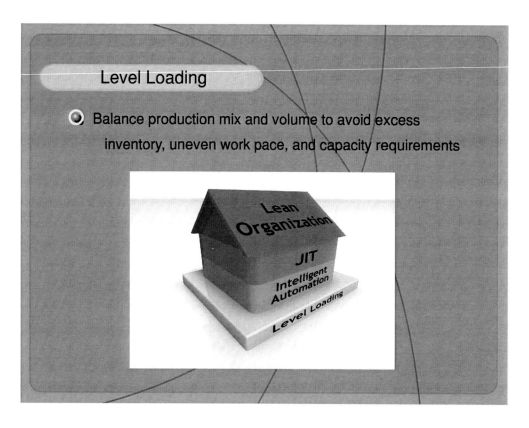

Notes, Slide 28:

_____

_____

_____

_____

_____

_____

Level Loading

- Adapting production rates to variation in customer demand
    - Variation in volume
    - Variation in product mix
    - Maintain constant staffing

- Leveling allows production of a variety of products smoothly throughout each day, week, and month

Notes, Slide 29:

Tip:
Leve loading pro-
civdes the motivation
to reduce a number
of activities, such as
assembly time, setup
time, and order entry
time.

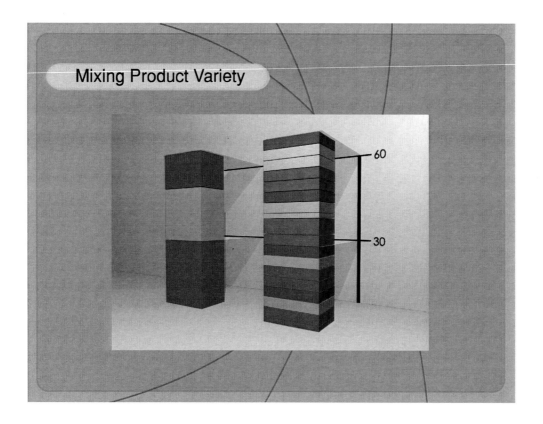

Notes, Slide 30:

_____

_____

_____

_____

_____

_____

Question:

Can you see any other benefit to the goal of producing in smaller batches?

_____

_____

_____

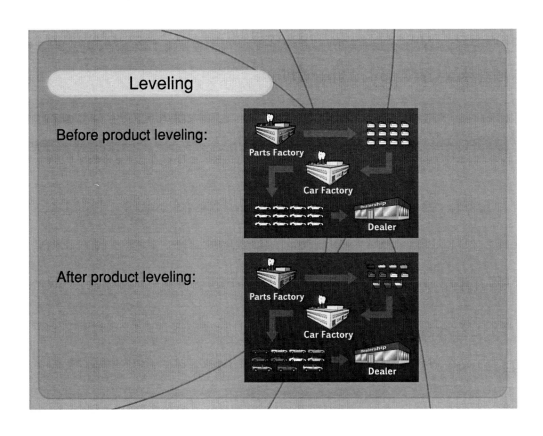

Notes, Slide 31:

_____

_____

_____

_____

_____

_____

Question:

What are the advantages of this type of system?

_____

_____

_____

Level Loading Benefits

- Less Work-In-Process inventory
- Production is agile to customer demands
- More consistent work due to variety in production
- Less fluctuation in capacity requirements
- Less Finished Goods inventory
- Avoids excess Finished Goods inventory

Notes, Slide 32:

_____

_____

_____

_____

_____

_____

Conclusions:

_____

_____

_____

_____

Suggestion:

Take a few minutes to write down any comments, conclusions, or concepts that you have learned during this section of the presentation.

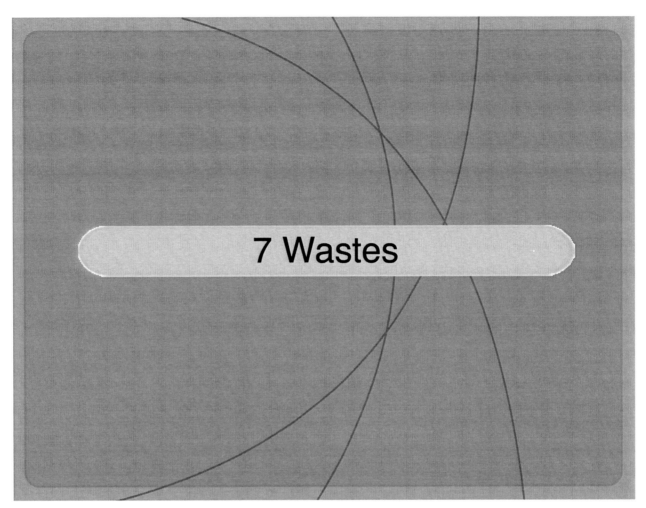

7 Wastes

Participant Workbook

In this Section

- Lean Manufacturing and the 7 Wastes
- Understanding the 7 Wastes
- Study the components of Lean
- Understand the Workshop Content

 Suggestion   **Tip**   **Question**

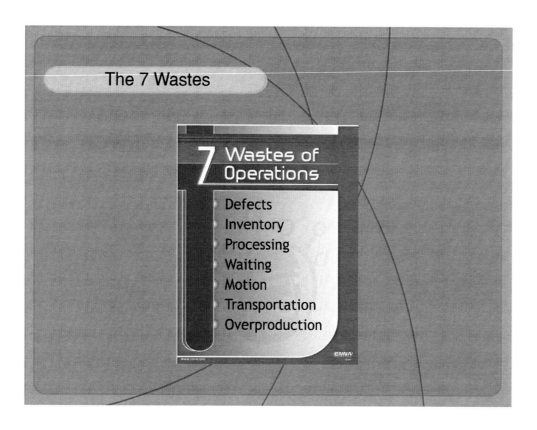

The 7 Wastes

7 Wastes of Operations

Defects
Inventory
Processing
Waiting
Motion
Transportation
Overproduction

Notes, Slide 34:

Tip:
The 7 Wastes are a fundamental building block of Lean. Ask the facilitator to fully explain the wastes so tha tyou understand them completely.

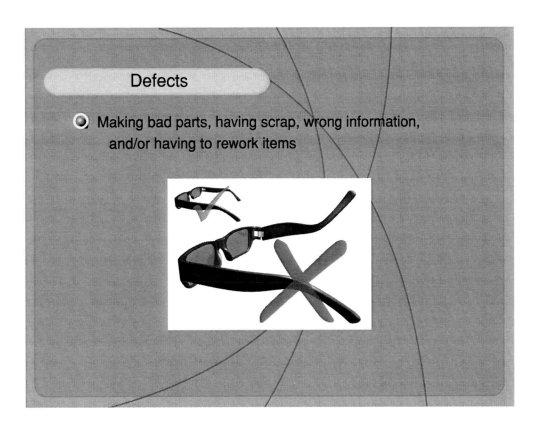

Notes, Slide 35:

_____

_____

_____

_____

Waste Definition: _____

_____

Additional Example: _____

_____

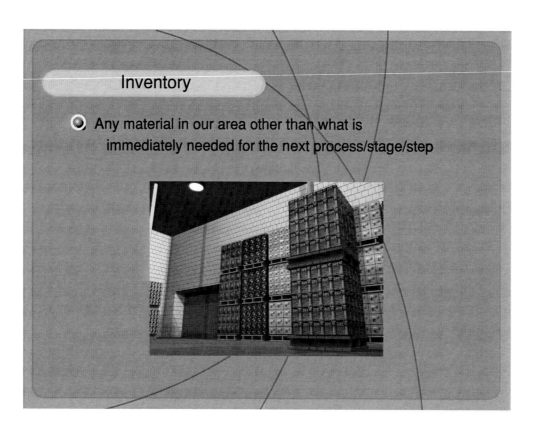

Inventory

- Any material in our area other than what is immediately needed for the next process/stage/step

Notes, Slide 36:

_____

_____

_____

_____

Waste Definition: _____

_____

Additional Example: _____

_____

Question:

What are the three stages that inventory lives as in your company?

_____

_____

_____

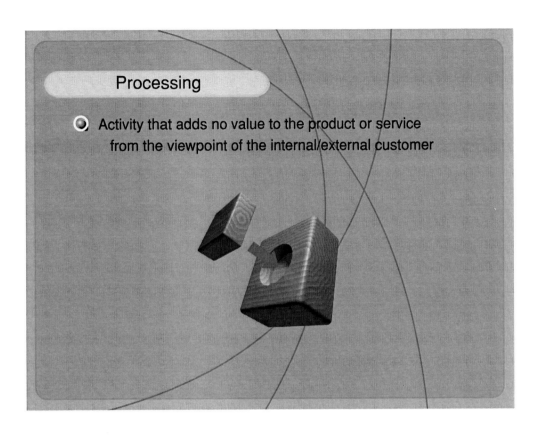

Processing

- Activity that adds no value to the product or service from the viewpoint of the internal/external customer

Notes, Slide 37:

_____

_____

_____

_____

_____

Tip:
This is the hardest waste to find, however the solution is simple. If you think about it, if it is truly a waste of processing then the ulti-mate solution is to find a way to not do it.

Waste Definition: _____

_____

Additional Example: _____

_____

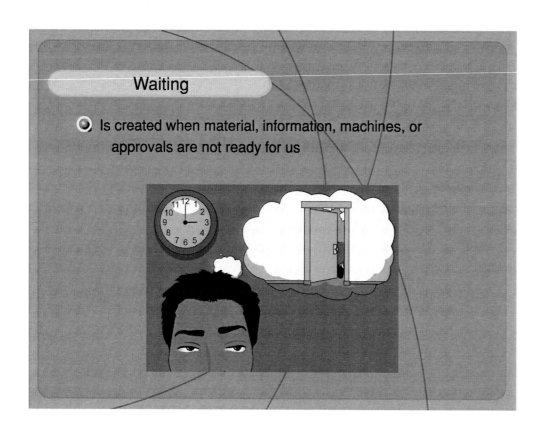

Waiting

- Is created when material, information, machines, or approvals are not ready for us

Notes, Slide 38:

_____

_____

_____

_____

Waste Definition: _____

_____

Suggestion:
Try purposely waiting for someone or something rather than doing something. It is hard to wait.

Additional Example: _____

_____

Question:

What are some times that you have waited, or when do you wait and what do you wait for?

_____

_____

_____

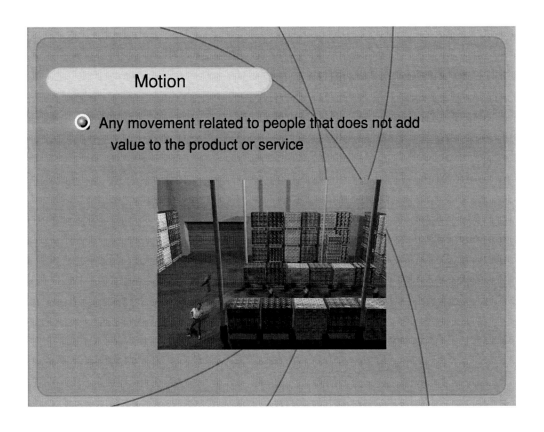

Notes, Slide 39:

_____

_____

_____

_____

Waste Definition: _____

_____

Additional Example: _____

_____

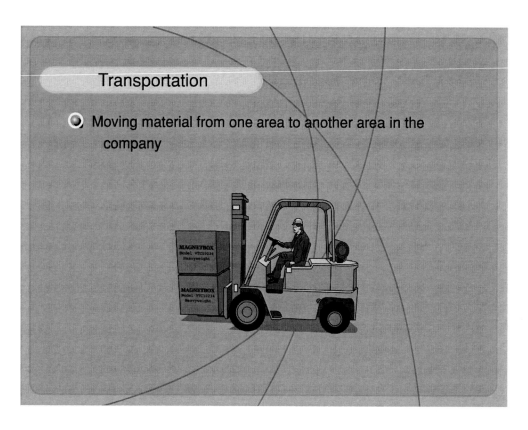

Transportation

○ Moving material from one area to another area in the
company

Notes, Slide 40:

_____

_____

_____

_____

Waste Definition: _____

_____

Additional Example: _____

_____

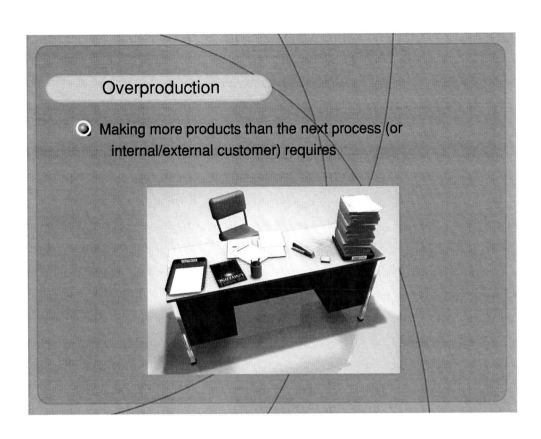

Notes, Slide 41:

_____

_____

_____

_____

_____

Tip:
Operations should look at ways to only produce what is truly needed. Anything more will result in loss of efficiency and effectiveness.

Waste Definition: _____

_____

Additional Example: _____

_____

Question:
Why do you think we give overproduction such a high score?

_____

_____

_____

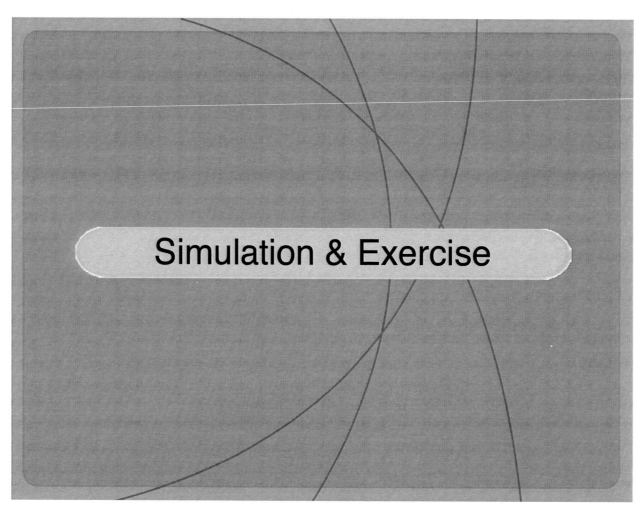

Simulation & Exercise

Participant Workbook

In this Section

- A guide to Flow Simulation
- The 7 Wastes Observation Exercise

 Suggestion   **Tip**   **Question**

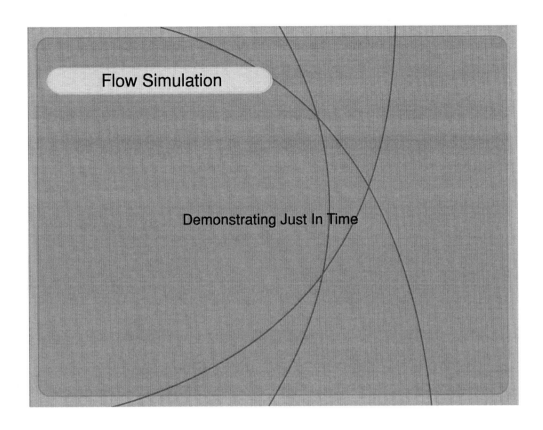

Notes, Slide 43:

Notes, Slide 44:

_____

_____

_____

_____

_____

_____

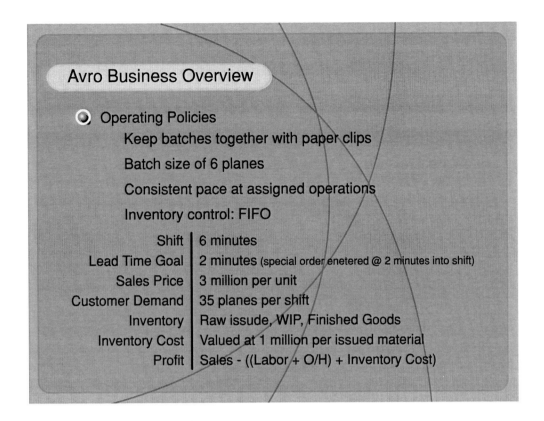

Avro Business Overview

- Operating Policies
    - Keep batches together with paper clips
    - Batch size of 6 planes
    - Consistent pace at assigned operations
    - Inventory control: FIFO

Shift	6 minutes
Lead Time Goal	2 minutes (special order enetered @ 2 minutes into shift)
Sales Price	3 million per unit
Customer Demand	35 planes per shift
Inventory	Raw issude, WIP, Finished Goods
Inventory Cost	Valued at 1 million per issued material
Profit	Sales - ((Labor + O/H) + Inventory Cost)

Notes, Slide 45:

_____

_____

_____

_____

_____

_____

Tip:
Although each pertici-pant will have a specific task, also consider how the inventory is moving from one process to the next process.

Production Schedule

- Production Batch
    - Batch of 6 airplanes per SKU

- Special Order
    - Detailing a special colored star on a wingtip

- Changeover (Setup)
    - After every 6 airplanes, fold setup paper one time
    - (except for Op10)

Notes, Slide 46:

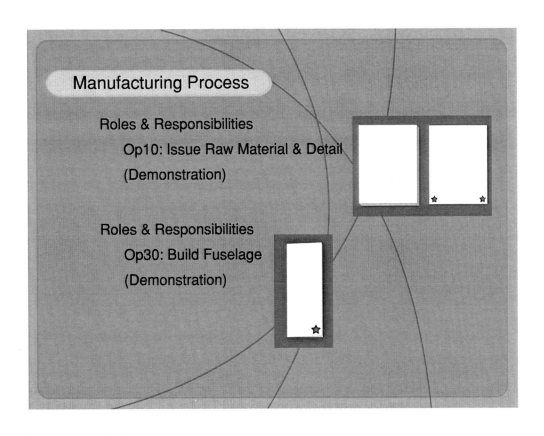

Notes, Slide 47:

_____

_____

_____

_____

_____

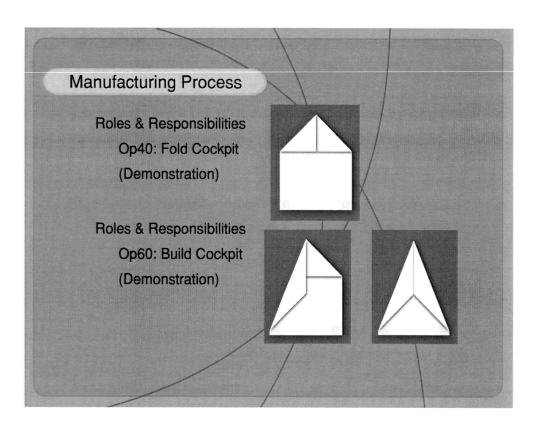

Notes, Slide 48:

_____

_____

_____

_____

_____

_____

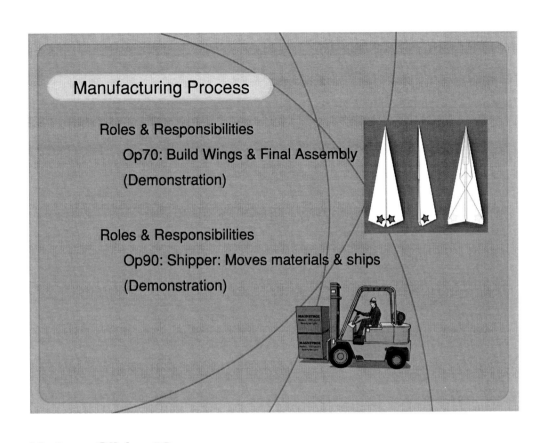

Notes, Slide 49:

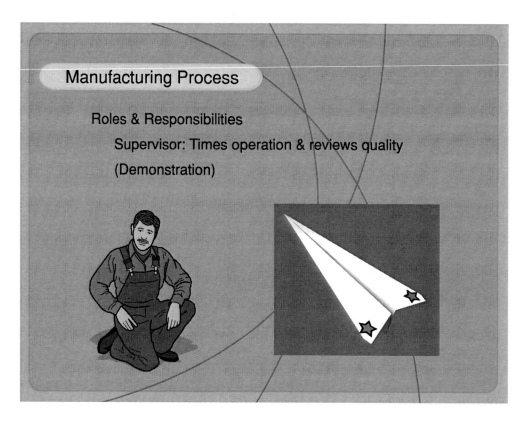

Notes, Slide 50:

_____

_____

_____

_____

_____

_____

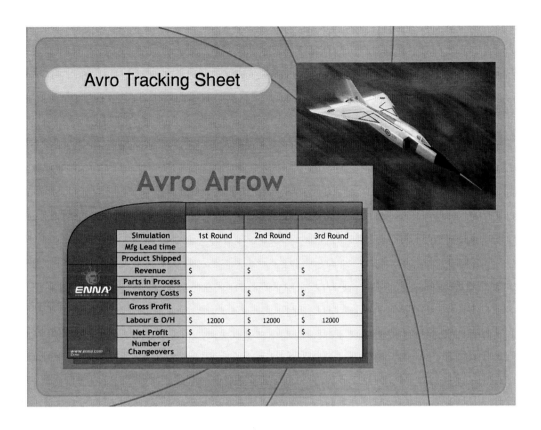

Avro Tracking Sheet

Avro Arrow

Simulation	1st Round	2nd Round	3rd Round
Mfg Lead time			
Product Shipped			
Revenue	$	$	$
Parts in Process			
Inventory Costs	$	$	$
Gross Profit			
Labour & O/H	$ 12000	$ 12000	$ 12000
Net Profit	$	$	$
Number of Changeovers			

Notes, Slide 51:

_____

_____

_____

_____

_____

_____

Question:

What observations did you make during the different stages of the simulation?

_____

_____

_____

_____

_____

Simulation

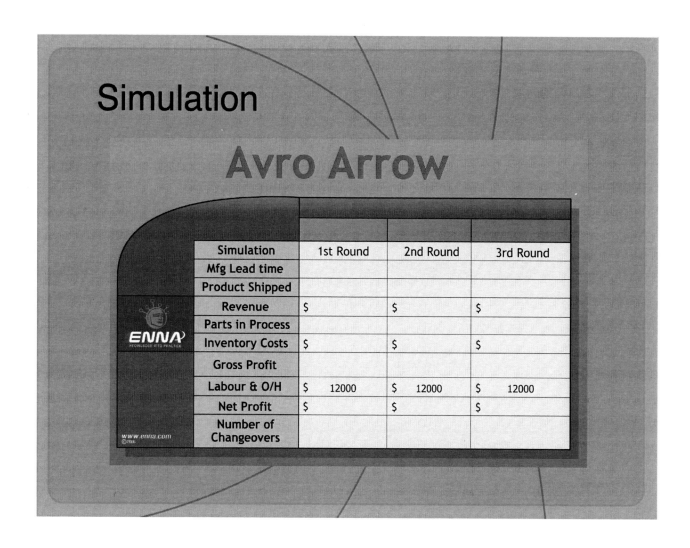

Simulation	1st Round	2nd Round	3rd Round
Mfg Lead time			
Product Shipped			
Revenue	$	$	$
Parts in Process			
Inventory Costs	$	$	$
Gross Profit			
Labour & O/H	$ 12000	$ 12000	$ 12000
Net Profit	$	$	$
Number of Changeovers			

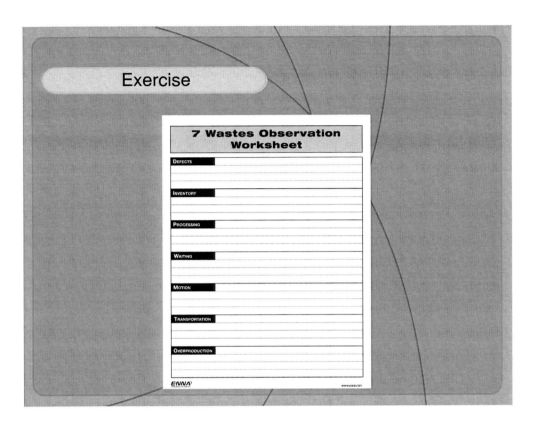

Exercise

7 Wastes Observation Worksheet

DEFECTS	
INVENTORY	
PROCESSING	
WAITING	
MOTION	
TRANSPORTATION	
OVERPRODUCTION	

ENNA

www.enna.com

Notes, Slide 52:

_____

_____

_____

_____

_____

_____

Tip:
For this exercise, work in teams of two people to discuss your observations.

Introduction to Lean Assessment

Facilitator: _____   Name: _____

Workshop: _____   Date: _____

Circle or write the answer that best fits the question or completes the statement.

1. _____ Lean was originally conceived by
   _____?
   a) James Womack
   b) Taiichi Ohno
   c) Shigeo Shingo

2. _____ What company started what is now
   known as Lean?
   a) Toyota
   b) Volvo
   c) General Motors

3. _____ What is the first element in JIT?
   a) Takt
   b) Flow
   c) Pull

4. _____ of the 7 Wastes of Operations
   which one is the worst?
   a) Motion
   b) Inventory
   c) Overproduction

5. _____ If a company does a good job with
   automation, the operator is more
   able to _____?
   a) not make mistakes
   b) multi-task
   c) take more breaks

6. _____ Lean is another word for _____?
   a) Intelligent Automation
   b) JIT
   c) Level Loading

7. _____ In business, Takt Time is _____.
   a) the amount of time it takes to make
      something
   b) the pace of customer demand
   c) total time for products to go through
      the facility

8. _____ What does inventory exist in the
   company as?
   a) Raw, WIP, FG
   b) GF, WIP, RAW
   c) PIW, WAR, FG

9. _____ In a Pull-based manufacturing system,
   who signals production?
   a) VP of Operations
   b) Production Manager
   c) Customer

10. _____ Intelligent Automation gives the machine
    _____.
    a) the ability to make good decisions
    b) the ability to decide what to make
    c) the ability to work autonomously

11. _____ Level Loading allows production of
    _____ each day, week, and month.
    a) a variety of products smoothly throughout
    b) few product varieties throughout
    c) large products with few variety throughout

12. _____ With an intelligent automation machine,
    the operator only has to _____.
    a) load and start the cycle
    b) inspect the part, load, and start the cycle
    c) unload and start the cycle

13. _____ What is the definition of a Flow production
    system in business terms?
    a) Everyone adds value when they want
    b) Moving the product from one process to
       the next without waiting
    c) Inventory will move from one place to the
       next and wait to be worked on

14. _____ Level Loading your operation will make
    it much easier to _____.
    a) make batches of materials
    b) minimize WIP inventory, less finished goods,
       and avoid fluctuations in capacity
    c) maximize WIP inventory, produce more
       finished goods, and increase fluctuations
       in capacity

1:b, 2:a, 3:a, 4:c; 5:b, 6:b, 7:b, 8:a, 9:c, 10:c, 11:a, 12:a, 13:a, 14:b